Tyra Banks

Karen Schweitzer

Mason Crest Publishers

Produced by OTTN Publishing in association with
21st Century Publishing and Communications, Inc.

MASON CREST PUBLISHERS INC.
370 Reed Road
Broomall, Pennsylvania 19008
(866) MCP-BOOK (toll free)
www.masoncrest.com

Printed in the United States of America.

9 8 7 6 5 4 3 2

Library of Congress Cataloging-in-Publication Data

Schweitzer, Karen.
   Tyra Banks / Karen Schweitzer.
      p. cm. — (Modern role models)
   Includes bibliographical references and index.
ISBN 978-1-4222-0498-6 (hardcover) — ISBN 978-1-4222-0785-7 (pbk.)
   1. Banks, Tyra. 2. African American models—Biography—Juvenile literature.
3. Models (Person)—United States—Biography—Juvenile literature. 4. African
Americans in television broadcasting—Biography—Juvenile literature. I. Title.
HD6073.M772U567 2008
746.9'2092—dc22
[B]   2008025066

Publisher's note:
All quotations in this book come from original sources, and contain the spelling and grammatical inconsistencies of the original text.

CROSS-CURRENTS

*In the ebb and flow of the currents of life we are each influenced by many people, places, and events that we directly experience or have learned about. Throughout the chapters of this book you will come across **CROSS-CURRENTS** reference boxes. These boxes direct you to a **CROSS-CURRENTS** section in the back of the book that contains fascinating and informative sidebars and related pictures. Go on. ▶▶*

CONTENTS

1 America's Top Model   5

2 Growing Up Tyra   11

3 Inner and Outer Beauty   17

4 America's Next Top Host   27

5 Still on Top   37

Cross-Currents   46

Chronology   56

Accomplishments & Awards   57

Further Reading & Internet Resources   59

Glossary   60

Notes   61

Index   63

Picture Credits   64

About the Author   64

Lead judge and executive producer of the UPN show *America's Next Top Model*, Tyra Banks was on hand at the September 18, 2006, event launching a new network called The CW. Formed by the merger of CBS-owned UPN and Time Warner, The CW television network planned to broadcast Tyra's high-rated show in its prime-time lineup.

1

America's Top Model

TYRA BANKS HAS ESTABLISHED HERSELF AS ONE of the most famous **supermodels** in the world. She became a **runway** star at 17 years old and a household name at 21. Tyra's drive and ambition have made her one of the most influential women in television and a power player in the entertainment industry.

What many people don't realize is that there is more to Tyra than just a pretty face. She is a shrewd businesswoman and the head of a multimedia empire. In addition to Bankable Productions, her own film and television production company, Tyra owns Bankable Enterprises, a real estate and retail company. She has also created two hit television shows and enjoyed success in a number of different business ventures. Tyra is one of the few models who have been able to take their fame to the next level.

The fact that Tyra has made herself a household name was no accident. The self-made **mogul** planned her career carefully at the encouragement of her mother, Carolyn London-Johnson. She has worked to create a Tyra Banks "brand." This means that, because people are so familiar with her, Tyra's name or image can be used to sell clothes or fashion items, or to make people tune in to television programs on which she appears. In an interview with *Entertainment Weekly*, Tyra explained:

> **"Even as a model I used to think 'brand.' My mom always told me, 'Plan for the end at the beginning. You're gonna have to retire really early like an athlete, and then what are you gonna do after?' So I always looked at it knowing that there was something after. "**

➤ TOP MODEL SCORES ◀

Tyra began modeling at an early age, but modeling was never her first choice for a career. As a teenager, she had her heart set on working in film and television. A great deal of the success Tyra enjoys today is a direct result of that original dream.

In 2003, Tyra created a reality show called *America's Next Top Model*. The show brought young women together to compete for the title of America's Next Top Model and a modeling **contract**. Tyra acted as the show's host and **executive producer**. She also sat on a panel of judges that decided which models could remain in the running for the title each week and which models had to go home.

One of the show's goals was to introduce the real world of modeling to the mainstream population. From the start, Tyra knew this would be a challenge. She told *The Hollywood Reporter*:

> **"I understood that people really had no idea of what went into modeling, [that many people thought] it was without skill and all dependent on beauty. And nothing could be further from the truth. It's so much more than winning the genetic lottery. You have to be smart, carry yourself with confidence, work at it. "**

Although it may have been true that most people had no idea what it took to be a model, the general public certainly seemed interested in learning more. *America's Next Top Model* was an instant hit for the UPN network. The show's ratings were so high that it was renewed for a second season, and then a third. By the 2006–2007 television season, *America's Next Top Model* was the highest-rated series on The CW network, with more than 5.2 million people tuning in to watch Tyra every week.

CROSS-CURRENTS

To learn more about the global appeal of Tyra's show, read "America's Next Top Model Goes International." Go to page 46. ▶▶

A promotional poster for The CW's most-watched show, *America's Next Top Model*—often referred to as *ANTM* by its fans. During each season, or cycle, aspiring models receive training and tips on runway walking, acting, applying makeup, and other job requirements. They then compete in various challenges in an attempt to win a modeling contract.

➤ THE TYRA BANKS SHOW ⬅

America's Next Top Model is not Tyra's only television hit. She also serves as host of *The Tyra Banks Show*, a daytime talk show that debuted in 2005. By the end of the show's second season, more than 4.3 million women were watching Tyra each day as she interviewed celebrities and tackled **controversial** topics.

Most of the people who tuned in to *The Tyra Banks Show*—an estimated 90 percent—also watched *America's Next Top Model* each week. Network heads were impressed with the connection Tyra had with American women. She had one of the youngest and largest audiences in daytime television.

A second successful television program hosted by Tyra is her syndicated daytime talk show. *The Tyra Banks Show,* launched in September 2005, was originally taped in Los Angeles, California. Tyra later moved the show to New York. In this photograph taken before the beginning of the third season, she stands atop a New York City double-deck bus promoting the show's new home.

Critics and industry players noticed as well. At the end of its second season, *The Tyra Banks Show* had been nominated for six Daytime Emmy Awards, including Outstanding Talk Show and Outstanding Talk Show Host.

⇒ TYRA MOVES TO NEW YORK ⇐

The Tyra Banks Show had always been taped in Los Angeles, but in 2007, Tyra announced that the third season would be shot in New York City. Although she cited creative opportunities for the move, rumors surfaced that the show was moving so that she could be closer to her new boyfriend, investment banker John Utendahl. Tyra was quick to dismiss the gossip, saying:

> **"Moving the talk show to New York provides a great opportunity to meet all kinds of people and keep sharing the message of empowerment with everyone everywhere. The excitement of New York City will translate to the show each and every day as we continue to face compelling issues . . . head on."**

The Big Apple guest pool did bring a new energy to Tyra's show, which celebrated its 500th episode less than a year later. Guests ranging from the 2008 presidential candidates to kids from New York schools have appeared on *The Tyra Banks Show* since it moved to New York, and locals visit the studio every day for a chance to sit in the audience.

CROSS-CURRENTS

To find out about some other television shows filmed in the Big Apple, check out "Filming in New York City." Go to page 47. ▶▶

While growing up Tyra had problems with her body image—the way she felt about her appearance. In many interviews she has said that she felt too tall, too thin, and too awkward. Although the public would later hail Tyra as a glamorous supermodel, she says there was a time in her life when classmates made her feel painfully alone and out of place.

2

Growing Up Tyra

TYRA LYNNE BANKS WAS BORN ON DECEMBER 4, 1973, to Carolyn London and Donald Banks of Inglewood, California. She grew up in this suburb of Los Angeles with her parents and her older brother, Devin. Tyra's immediate family, as well as her grandparents, aunts, and other relatives, were a major influence in her life.

Both of Tyra's parents doted on her. Although Carolyn and Donald divorced when their daughter was six years old, they remained friendly and raised their children together. Tyra stayed with her mother during the week and with her father on the weekends. Tyra later said her parent's divorce didn't hurt or upset her in any way. She has said:

> **"**I admit I did fantasize sometimes about my parents getting back together. But as I got older, I realized that my parents were better off being

apart, and that my brother and I were happier because we weren't stuck in a house full of tension and anger. **"**

>> UGLY DUCKLING <<

Although Tyra's childhood was a happy time, her adolescence was not. She was plagued by dry skin, unsightly rashes, and other skin ailments. At the age of nine, she developed such a bad case of warts that she was afraid to show her hands to anyone. The kids at school began to call her "Froggy."

A growth spurt at age 11 made Tyra even more self-conscious about her looks. By the time she entered junior high school, she was five feet, nine inches tall—much taller than her fellow classmates and even some of her teachers. Tyra's brother and the kids at school teased her relentlessly for being so tall and skinny.

In Tyra's second year of junior high school, her parents decided to send her to Immaculate Heart Middle and High School, an all-girls private school in Los Angeles. Tyra did well at the private school and made quite a few new friends. As the years passed, she also became more confident and comfortable with her appearance. In her senior year, Tyra's high school friend Khefri convinced her to try modeling.

>> POUNDING THE PAVEMENT <<

Armed with a **portfolio** of pictures that had been shot by Carolyn, Tyra went to several different modeling agencies. One by one, each agency turned her away. Some said her look was "too ethnic." Others simply told her "thanks, but no thanks." Tyra's mother told *People Weekly* that skin color also played a factor:

"The market for black models was not very good. They would say, 'We have this many black girls already.'"

CROSS-CURRENTS
If you would like to learn about some other successful black models, read "Other African-American Super-models: Past and Present." Go to page 48. ▶▶

Tyra almost gave up the idea of modeling. She was interested in pursuing a career in film and television production and after graduating from high school in 1990 decided to enroll at Loyola Marymount University in Los Angeles. But three weeks before her freshman year started, Tyra's life took a drastic turn.

➤➤ STRUTTING THE RUNWAYS ⬅⬅

Encouraged by her mother, Tyra decided to visit one last agency: Elite Model Management. Elite was—and still is—one of the most prestigious modeling agencies in the world. The agency offered Tyra a modeling contract, and a Paris talent scout suggested that she put off college and give runway modeling a try.

Tyra was only 17 years old at the time. She had never traveled without her family and was both nervous and excited at the prospect of going to Paris. To prepare for the experience, she practiced posing

Tyra with her mother, Carolyn London. After her parents divorced in 1980, Tyra lived with her older brother and mother in a one-bedroom apartment in Inglewood, a suburb of Los Angeles. Tyra began to try breaking into the modeling business when she was around 15 years old. Carolyn served as her manager for the first seven years of her modeling career.

4th ANNIVERSARY SPECIAL!

P.O.V.

FOR MEN

THINK BIG!
7 WINNING RULES

SAMMY SOSA on Sportsmanship
STEVE CASE on Perseverance
LARRY FLYNT on Independence
NORMAN MAILER on Audacity
JOE TORRE on Patience
BEN BRADLEE on Truth

The Rise and Fall of an *NBA Rookie*

Wear a Suit Like an All-Star, p.96

APRIL 1999 • POINT OF VIEW

WIN A PRIZE A DAY!
www.povmag.com

TYRA BANKS

During the 1990s, Tyra found success on the runway and with advertising campaigns. She had a makeup contract with CoverGirl and appeared on the covers of numerous magazines. She was the first black supermodel to appear on the covers of several magazines, including *GQ* and the *Sports Illustrated* swimsuit issue.

and walking in her mom's high heels while she watched videotapes and fashion segments on TV.

Whatever Tyra did, it worked. She not only landed a magazine cover within her first two weeks in France, she was also booked for 25 fashion shows—a record for a new model.

Although there were many models at that time with rags-to-riches stories, Tyra's success was **unprecedented**. She quickly became the new queen of the runway as more and more designers began to request her on the **catwalk**.

➤ FROM MODEL TO ACTRESS ◄

In 1991, Tyra began to expand her career into acting roles. First, she appeared in a series of music videos, including Michael Jackson's *Black or White* and Tina Turner's *Love Thing*. She also appeared in George Michael's *Too Funky* video and a British TV movie called *Inferno*. Her big break came less than a year later, when she was cast as Will Smith's girlfriend in several episodes of his television show, *The Fresh Prince of Bel-Air*.

In 1995, Tyra made her big-screen debut in *Higher Learning*. The movie was directed by her boyfriend at the time, John Singleton. Both Tyra and the movie received good reviews, cementing her status as a promising actress.

CROSS-CURRENTS

Read "Crossing Over into Acting" to learn about other models who have succeeded in the entertainment world. Go to page 49. ▶▶

➤ BREAKING BARRIERS ◄

That same year, Tyra added more than 20 European magazine covers and a handful of American covers to her résumé. With the help of her mother, who was now her manager as well, Tyra also negotiated a **lucrative** contract with CoverGirl Cosmetics. This was a major achievement. Up to this point, only one other African-American model had been under contract with this major cosmetics company.

The following year, Tyra accomplished another great feat. She became the first African-American model to appear alone on the cover of the *Sports Illustrated* swimsuit issue. That same year, she also became the first African-American woman to appear on the covers of *GQ* and the *Victoria's Secret* catalog. The triple achievement made her one of the most recognized models in the world.

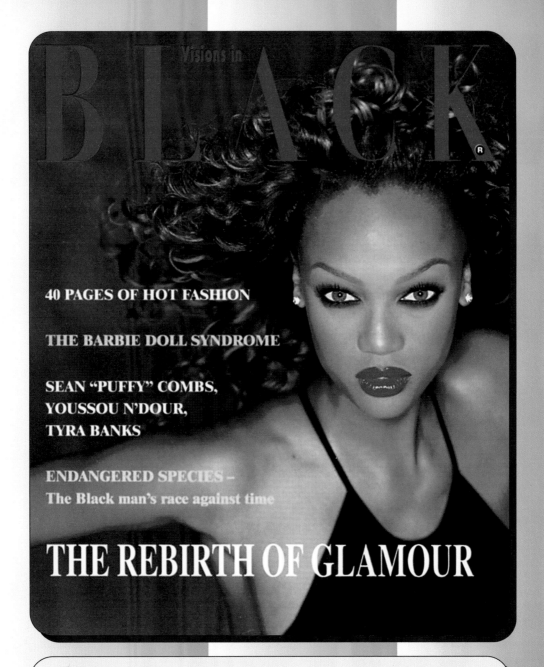

Visions in

BLACK ®

40 PAGES OF HOT FASHION

THE BARBIE DOLL SYNDROME

SEAN "PUFFY" COMBS,
YOUSSOU N'DOUR,
TYRA BANKS

ENDANGERED SPECIES –
The Black man's race against time

THE REBIRTH OF GLAMOUR

Tyra Banks poses on the cover of *Visions in Black*. It didn't take long for the fledgling model to turn into a supermodel— one of the top fashion models whose good looks, or outer beauty, bring top salaries and celebrity. Supermodels are typically in high demand as magazine cover girls, in advertising campaigns, and in top fashion shows.

3

Inner and Outer Beauty

MAKING IT ONTO THE COVER OF THREE MAJOR fashion magazines in the same year made Tyra one of the most visible models in the world. It was not long before her image was plastered everywhere. She was featured in advertisements for McDonald's, Nike, Pepsi-Cola, and other major corporations. Tyra also appeared on a number of television and awards shows.

In the spring of 1997, Tyra was featured in three episodes of *New York Undercover*, an award-winning television drama. She played Natasha Claybourne, a French teacher who becomes involved with one of the show's lead characters.

That same year, Tyra also starred in the independent film *A Woman Like That*. The movie premiered at the Urbanworld Film Festival and was awarded the title of "Best Dramatic Feature." *A Woman Like That* took only 24 days to film, but it generated a lot of buzz about Tyra's acting talent.

➤ VALIDATION ⤺

Tyra also received validation for modeling in 1997 when she won the Michael Award for Supermodel of the Year. The Michael Awards, sometimes called the "Oscars of Fashion," recognize the people who exert the greatest influence on the fashion world.

The annual awards ceremony doubles as a benefit for the National Children's Leukemia Foundation, an organization that supports research and programs for children and adults with leukemia, a cancer that affects the blood and bone marrow. Some of the other models honored with the prestigious Supermodel of the Year award include Lydia Hearst, Carmen Kass, and Karolina Kurkova.

Tyra added a second trophy to her collection that year when she won the Supermodel of the Year award at the 1997 VH1 Fashion and Music Awards.

➤ GIVING BACK ⤺

Tyra's newfound celebrity status offered her many different opportunities. She took advantage of her fame to influence her fans to help people in need. At Christmastime, she sponsored toy drives and encouraged others to give both their time and their money to gather gifts for children.

Tyra also gave guest lectures at Johns Hopkins University, Howard University, Georgetown University, the University of Houston, and a number of other schools and kids camps. Her lectures covered topics ranging from self-esteem and empowerment for women to education and the environment.

When Tyra wasn't collecting toys or giving lectures, she was working with one of her favorite charities, the Center for Children and Family. The Center, which is dedicated to helping neglected and abused children, enlisted Tyra as a **spokesperson**. She helped to promote a line of greeting cards for the organization and also acted as a mentor to at-risk kids. Tyra said it was the children who inspired her to volunteer her time:

> **"I truly get so much satisfaction out of spending time with the kids. They're like my surrogate children. We read together and paint together and every Valentine's Day they give me a huge stack of cards— I've wallpapered one wall in my house with them."**

➤ TYRA'S CHARITIES ◀

Tyra has made an effort to share not only her time, but also her wealth, with others. In 1992, she established the Tyra Banks Scholarship. The **scholarship** program is an annual fund that helps girls pay the tuition to attend Tyra's alma mater, Immaculate Heart High

Tyra poses with the school principal of Immaculate Heart, as she presents a donation to the scholarship fund that she established at the school. The scholarship program provides funding for African-American girls to attend the Catholic, all-girl, college preparatory school located in Los Angeles, California. Tyra graduated from the high school in 1990.

School. Girls who win the scholarship have the opportunity to take classes, play sports, and enjoy the many resources that Immaculate Heart is known for.

In July 1999, Tyra created the TZONE Foundation, which sponsors summer camps for disadvantaged teenage girls. The mission of the annual TZONE camp experience was self-empowerment—teaching young women how to be confident in their abilities and decisions. Those who attended camp had the chance to develop leadership skills and work through issues related to their self-esteem. They also got to hang out with Tyra, who acted as a counselor. She described her role in an interview with *Redbook*:

> **"I tell the girls of my experiences growing up—how it was difficult for me, too. A lot of them are shocked when they see me shed tears about the things I'm not happy with about myself."**

CROSS-CURRENTS

For some additional information about the good works performed by Tyra's charitable foundation, read "Tyra's TZONE." Go to page 50. ▶▶

In its first three years, TZONE helped more than 200 girls in California. The success of TZONE eventually prompted Tyra to make the foundation a national charity.

 ## BEAUTY INSIDE AND OUT

By the mid-1990s, Tyra had become well known for her ability to strike a pose on the runway, as well as for her charitable work. However, few people realized she had writing talents as well. In 1996, she began working on a book on beauty and self-confidence with fashion writer Vanessa Thomas Bush.

Two years later, the book hit the stores. *Tyra's Beauty Inside and Out* was meant to serve as a response to the millions of questions Tyra received from fans each year about makeup, exercise, modeling, and dating. In the book, she shares the beauty tips and tricks she has learned from experts over the years, as well as personal life stories.

Tyra's Beauty Inside and Out also addressed serious issues like drug abuse, the unhappiness many people feel about their bodies, and romantic relationships. In her introduction to the book, Tyra wrote:

66 There are a million books out there that tell you how to apply lipstick, but I wanted to lay it all out on what really makes a woman beautiful, and I wanted to be open and honest on everything from sex and dating to substance abuse to self-empowerment. 99

Although she became a celebrity because of her glamorous looks, Tyra has often said that she believes what lies within a person is more important than what appears on the outside. Her book, *Tyra's Beauty Inside & Out,* published in 1998, is a self-help book aimed at helping girls and young women develop self-esteem.

Tyra's book was received well by critics, who gave it good reviews. CoverGirl Cosmetics also helped to cross-promote *Tyra's Beauty Inside and Out* by enclosing coupons for the company's products and funding some of the stops on Tyra's book tour.

⋙ YOUTH CORRESPONDENT ⋘

Shortly after her book was released, Tyra began working as a youth **correspondent** for *The Oprah Winfrey Show*. She was thrilled about the prospect of working with Oprah Winfrey. Tyra had always admired the famous talk-show hostess.

CROSS-CURRENTS

If you would like to learn more about one of Tyra's own role models, read "Getting to Know Oprah." Go to page 50. ▶▶

Tyra's job on Oprah's show involved interviewing guests and at times, co-hosting the show. Some of the topics Tyra covered in her two years with *The Oprah Winfrey Show* include makeovers, exercise, and family relations. Oprah complimented the work Tyra did. She often told viewers that Tyra was a rising star, and that they would see more of her in the future.

⋙ MOVIE STAR ⋘

As it turned out, Oprah was right. Between 1999 and 2001, Tyra appeared in several movies. Instead of taking the first scripts offered, however, Tyra choose her roles carefully. She wanted to be taken seriously as an actress, and not considered just a pretty face. It was important to pick the right films.

One of the first movies in which Tyra appeared was *The Apartment Complex*. Tyra only had a few scenes in the 1999 Showtime thriller, but she made a big impression on viewers. Later in the year, she had a small part in the big-screen comedy *Love Stinks* with French Stewart and Bill Bellamy.

In 2000, Tyra added more acting credits to her résumé by appearing in several other movies, including the critically acclaimed film *Love & Basketball*. The movie tells the story of a female basketball player who finds love with a childhood friend. *Love & Basketball*, which was produced by Spike Lee, reunited Tyra with her *Higher Learning* costar Omar Epps.

That same year, Tyra starred with Lindsay Lohan in the Disney television movie *Life-Size*. The movie garnered huge ratings for Disney and great reviews for Tyra. A few months after the television movie aired, Tyra appeared in *Coyote Ugly*. Her character, Zoë, was part of a team of girls who worked as bartenders and dancers in a New York hangout. *Coyote Ugly* was one of the most anticipated films of the summer and a huge hit at the box office.

⇒ VICTORIA'S SECRET ANGEL ⇐

Between her acting jobs, Tyra continued her modeling career. One of the companies she worked for regularly was Victoria's Secret. Tyra signed a long-term contract with the women's **lingerie** company after gracing the cover of one of its catalogs.

The Victoria's Secret Angels made their debut at the women's wear and lingerie company's 1999 fashion show. In this November 11, 2004, photograph taken in Miami Beach Florida, they are signing autographs during the Victoria's Secret "Angels Across America" cross-country tour. From left to right are Tyra Banks, Adriana Lima, Alessandra Ambrosio, Heidi Klum, and Gisele Bundchen.

Tyra also made frequent appearances in print ads for the company and became a Victoria's Secret Angel in 1999. Angels are Victoria Secret's most visible models; some also act as spokeswomen. Tyra and the rest of the Victoria's Secret Angels—including supermodels Heidi Klum, Rebecca Romijn, and Adriana Lima—made their debut that year at the company's fourth annual fashion show. The Angels all wore lingerie and huge feathered wings. People couldn't stop talking about the event or the Angels, prompting Victoria's Secret to keep the promotional idea going.

Tyra Banks and rapper Busta Rhymes appear in a scene from *Halloween: Resurrection*, released in the summer of 2002. The slasher movie is the eighth installment of a series of films based on *Halloween* (1978), a film in which a stalker murders teenage babysitters on Halloween Night. *Halloween: Resurrection* also starred Jamie Lee Curtis and Brad Loree.

In 2001, the company inked a deal with ABC to broadcast its annual fashion show on television. The show's TV debut that November drew millions of viewers, but also stirred up controversy. The Federal Communications Commission, the U.S. government agency that regulates radio and television broadcasting, received numerous complaints about the show. Some groups, like the National Organization for Women, staged protests during the broadcast to express their displeasure. However, not everyone disapproved. There were a number of feminist groups that stepped forward to support Tyra and the other models.

TYRA'S LOVE LIFE

Although Tyra was busy with acting and modeling, she still found time to date. After her three-year relationship with film director John Singleton ended, Tyra dated the British singer Seal for a brief period. In 2002, however, she found love with NBA player Chris Webber, who played basketball at the time for the Sacramento Kings.

For the next few years, Tyra often sat courtside when the Kings were in town and sometimes traveled with Chris when the team was on the road. Their relationship was very serious and most people assumed that it was only a matter of time before the couple married.

NEW PROJECTS

Not surprisingly, 2002 was another whirlwind year for Tyra. She had dozens of projects in the works, including parts in two movies. In the horror movie *Halloween: Resurrection*, Tyra was one of several characters who are murdered by psycho killer Michael Myers. Critics weren't fond of the movie, but it captured more than $30 million at the box office.

Although *Halloween: Resurrection* didn't get rave reviews, *Eight Crazy Nights* did. Tyra had a small part, lending her voice to this Adam Sandler cartoon. It was the first time she had ever voiced an animated character for a major Hollywood movie, but she handled the job like a pro.

Tyra poses at a UPN event held in New York, May 19, 2005. At that time, her show *America's Next Top Model* was syndicated in more than 100 countries. Tyra's success with her first show with UPN made network executives willing to take a second look when she pitched the idea for a talk show that she wanted to host.

America's Next Top Host

THE PROJECT THAT WOULD CHANGE TYRA'S LIFE started in her kitchen during 2002. She was making a cup of tea when the idea hit her: why not create a reality show that follows wannabe supermodels as they try to win a modeling contract? Tyra was sure that the idea had potential. All she had to do was convince everyone else.

The first person Tyra spoke to was her agent. They talked about the project several times, but the agent kept insisting that nobody would be interested in watching a show about models. Unwilling to give up on the idea, Tyra went to a writer friend who eventually introduced her to agent Ken Mok.

Ken had experience developing and producing reality shows, and he thought that Tyra's idea had merit. The two began working out how they would **pitch** the show to other people. Tyra knew it might not be an easy sell.

Tyra took the idea to the CBS network first, then to UPN. Dawn Ostroff, the former entertainment president of UPN, admitted later to *Entertainment Weekly* that at first the network wasn't very interested:

> **"It was kind of a courtesy pitch. Many times people have ideas who haven't worked in television, and you always take the pitch because you never know where a hit can come from. Tyra totally understood how to entertain when she pitched the show."**

⟫ THE GREEN LIGHT ⟪

After hearing Tyra's proposal, UPN ordered eight episodes of the reality show, which was tentatively titled *Supermodel*. Network executives were eager to get the show on the air, so work began immediately. The tight schedule gave Tyra and the casting team less than a month to sort through 1,000 applications to find suitable contestants for the first season. She also had to find judges and experts who were willing to appear on the show.

Tyra was able to draw on her contacts in the modeling industry. Longtime friend Kimora Lee Simmons, former supermodel Janice Dickinson, and *Marie Claire* fashion editor Beau Quillian all agreed to be judges for the first season. Tyra also managed to hire a runway coach, makeup artists, and other crewmembers in the nick of time.

The premise of *Supermodel*—later renamed *America's Next Top Model*—was both simple and exciting. Cameras would follow 10 beautiful girls as they competed for a modeling contract. The models were expected to participate in challenging photo shoots and other exercises. After each event the panel of judges would critique the girls. The judges would send one girl home each week. The last model standing would win a contract with Wilhelmina Models, a contract with Revlon Cosmetics, and a photo spread in *Marie Claire* magazine. To keep things exciting, all of the models were required to live together in a small apartment for the duration of the show.

It took approximately eight weeks to film the first season of *America's Next Top Model*. There weren't always enough crewmembers available to run the camera, so Ken Mok, Tyra, and the rest of the production team filled in whenever necessary.

Executive producer Tyra Banks talks with Jay Manuel, makeup artist and director of photo-shoots on *American's Next Top Model*. The Canadian-born fashion photographer, who also serves as Tyra's personal makeup artist, hosts and is lead judge for a spin-off of *ANTM* broadcast in Canada. On *ANTM*, he is commonly referred to as "Mister Jay."

FIRST SEASON SUCCESS

When *America's Next Top Model* debuted, nobody noticed that it had been put together on a tight budget within a limited time frame. The show was an instant success for the UPN network. Viewers tuned in every week to watch the drama unfold.

The contestants took the show seriously, realizing that winning it would provide many modeling opportunities. Adrianne Curry, a 20-year-old waitress from a small town in Illinois, eventually became the first winner of *America's Next Top Model*. The title gave her modeling career the boost it needed. After winning, Adrienne went on to appear in many magazine advertisements.

UPN announced in November 2003 that it would renew *America's Next Top Model* for a second season. The first season of the show had been the highest-rated UPN program among women viewers, and the network was hoping for repeat success.

BANKABLE PRODUCTIONS

Tyra was not just interested in putting her name on products like *America's Next Top Model*. She wanted to have control. In 2003, she decided to form Bankable Productions, her own production company. Bankable Productions started out with 10 employees, and its first job was producing the second season of *America's Next Top Model*. The company came up with a new catchphrase for the show: "They are all gorgeous, but only one has what it takes."

CROSS-CURRENTS
For more on the work Tyra does producing her television shows, read "Tyra's Work Behind the Camera." Go to page 52.

There were a few changes for season two. There were 12 contestants instead of 10, and the panel of judges changed. Although Tyra and Janice Dickinson remained, Kimora Lee Simmons and Beau Quillian were replaced with photographer Nigel Barker and magazine editor Eric Nicholson.

Like the contestants from season one, the season two models lived together in one house. They competed in a number of different challenges and were eliminated one by one. Yoanna House, a 23-year-old aspiring model from Florida, eventually earned the title of America's Next Top Model.

SHAKE YA BODY

The success of *America's Next Top Model* enabled Tyra to try to move into another area in which she had always been interested: popular

Alexander Jenkins, referred to as J. Alexander, sits next to Tyra as both judge *American's Next Top Model* contestants. J. Alexander is a model and runway coach, whose success on ANTM has made him a television celebrity. A longtime friend of Tyra's, Alexander is known as "King of the Catwalk."

music. She had taken singing and dancing lessons for years, and her singing had been featured in several of her movies. Before the second season of *Top Model* ended, Tyra asked six of the contestants to appear in a video for a song that she wanted to release. The name of the song and the video, which would premiere on UPN, was "Shake Ya Body."

Right before Tyra's video came out, she told *The New York Times* that she would release her own CD in the fall of 2004:

> **"I've been singing for six years, but I never wanted to talk to the press about it. I felt that coming from the modeling world, people don't tend**

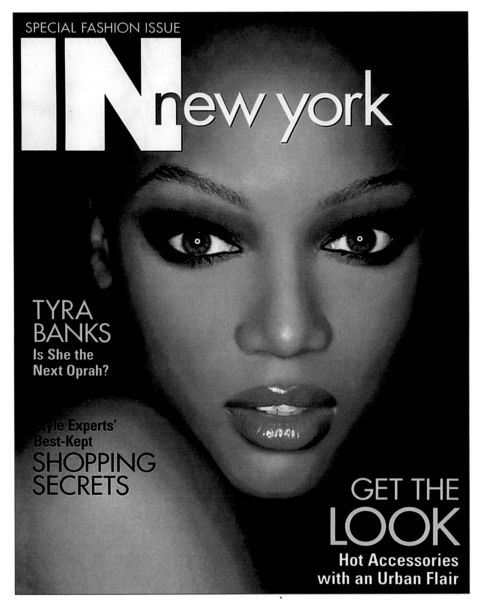

SPECIAL FASHION ISSUE

IN new york

TYRA
BANKS
Is She the
Next Oprah?

Style Experts'
Best-Kept
SHOPPING
SECRETS

GET THE
LOOK
Hot Accessories
with an Urban Flair

Tyra appears on the cover of *In New York*'s September 2005 issue. She had just launched her new talk show and one magazine headline was already asking whether Tyra Banks was the next Oprah. Many critics believe Tyra's appeal to younger audiences will allow her to become just as influential as the longtime host of *The Oprah Winfrey Show.*

to take us seriously. And I totally understand that. So I wanted to make sure that my stuff was tight, that my voice was tight, that my dancing was tight. **"**

"Shake Ya Body" was meant to be a taste of the kind of music Tyra planned on putting out, but the single was a flop. The failure prompted her to cancel her CD plans and focus on other projects.

➤ TYRA GETS A TALK SHOW ◀

Tyra may have been unable to get her music career off the ground, but that did not stop her from trying new things. In late 2004, she made a deal with Telepictures Productions and Warner Bros. Domestic Television Distribution to star in a syndicated talk show.

Telepictures president Jim Paratore told *The Hollywood Reporter* that Tyra's appeal, as well as her previous work experience on *The Oprah Winfrey Show* and *America's Next Top Model*, helped convince the television executives that she could succeed with a talk show:

> **"**She's really emerged as a role model for the next generation of young women. She has a feel for this generation of women, and she's worked with women for a long time. I think that's a big part of what's driving her. **"**

The idea to do a talk show had been in Tyra's head since her days as a youth correspondent on *The Oprah Winfrey Show*. She had been offered her own show when her correspondent job ended but had turned it down. In an interview with *Redbook*, she explained why she didn't seize the original opportunity:

> **"**I thought I was too young, and hadn't experienced enough. And I was probably judgmental back then. I hadn't experienced real heartbreak. **"**

Tyra had suffered real heartbreak earlier in the year when her relationship with boyfriend Chris Webber ended after two years. Because she envisioned a talk show that focused on issues facing women, Tyra had plenty of material from her personal life, as well as her professional life, to share with an audience.

➤ TALK SHOW DEBUT ◄

When *The Tyra Banks Show* premiered on September 12, 2005, a lot of people wondered whether Tyra would be able to cut it as a talk show host. She had just finished filming seasons three and four of *America's Next Top Model*, and was already busy working with Bankable Productions on the fifth season. Creating a successful talk show is not easy. About 90 percent of new talk shows get cancelled within their first two years.

But once again Tyra showed that she could do more than just look good while walking down a runway. Her talk show was a big hit in its first year. She benefited from publicity on *America's Next Top Model*, which helped draw her fans to the new program. However, they kept coming back because of the interesting topics that Tyra discussed every week. Unlike some talk shows, Tyra's show focused more on women's issues than on celebrities. The strategy paid off in higher ratings. This helped to get *The Tyra Banks Show* renewed for two more years when the program was still in its first season.

The show's success gave Tyra's Bankable Productions a chance to develop projects like movies, other television shows, and online ventures. Most of these projects were very different, but they all had a common purpose: to empower and inspire young girls and women.

CROSS-CURRENTS

For information about some other female talk show hosts who have become very successful, read "Other Women's Talk Shows." Go to page 53. ▶▶

➤ TYRA RETIRES FROM MODELING ◄

In 2005, Tyra officially retired from modeling. Many people were surprised by this decision because she was still one of the most in-demand models in the industry. She had a $4 million modeling contract with Victoria's Secret and could earn up to $50,000 per day on photo shoots.

But Tyra knew she wouldn't have time for modeling with two television shows and other projects in the works. She also wanted to retire when she was still on top.

For her last walk down the runway, Tyra chose the annual Victoria's Secret fashion show broadcast that December. In an interview before the show, she commented on her retirement:

❝I'm not just retiring from the runway, I'm retiring from all modeling. . . . When I was 18, my mom said

Tyra Banks and Alessandra Ambrosio, both members of Victoria's Secret Angels, serve as spokeswomen promoting the company's latest fragrance in this 2005 photograph. In addition to offering fashion-inspired collections of women's apparel and lingerie, Victoria's Secret also sells perfumes, home fragrances, and prestige beauty products.

I have to have a plan. I decided I'd leave on top. I want to be like the athletes who seem stuck in time. When you see them at 50, you say they probably can still run like a champ.”

Tyra on location during shooting for an upcoming episode of *America's Next Top Model*. Staying on top has meant keeping to a demanding schedule. She has been known to wake up at 4 a.m., work 12 hours a day, seven days a week, in order to tape two talk-show episodes three days a week, as well as daily segments for *ANTM.*

5

Still on Top

AT THE BEGINNING OF 2006, TYRA HAD MANY projects underway. *America's Next Top Model* was beginning its sixth season and was more popular than ever. But there were questions about whether or not the show could continue. UPN, the network that broadcast *America's Next Top Model*, was shutting down.

Executives at CBS, which owned UPN, decided to merge the network with The WB, another small network that was owned by Warner Brothers. In September 2006 a brand-new television network called The CW was launched. Because *Top Model* had been one of UPN's highest-rated shows, it was transferred to The CW. In fact, the premiere of the seventh season of *America's Next Top Model* was the first new show aired on The CW, on September 20, 2006.

⇒ SOPHOMORE SEASON ⇐

After making sure that *America's Next Top Model* had a new home on The CW network, Tyra was able to concentrate on her talk show, which was entering its second season.

The show was doing well—drawing more than 2 million viewers per week—but it wasn't exactly where Tyra wanted it to be yet. She planned to tackle more controversial topics in the second season. She also wanted to work on becoming a better speaker and a more effective listener.

During the summer, Tyra took classes with a coach to improve her hosting skills. The lessons were an absolute necessity, she explained:

> **For the first season of the talk show, I would scream high-pitched and do a lot of stupid things. Or, I'd interview someone and they'd say something poignant, but I wouldn't hear because I was so focused on my next question. So, I learned to listen and have it be a conversation.**

Tyra's efforts to improve her show and her hosting seemed to work. The second season of *The Tyra Banks Show* was nominated for a Prism Award, an NAACP Image Award, and a GLAAD Award. The show also received six Daytime Emmy Award **nominations**, including Outstanding Talk Show Host and Outstanding Talk Show. Tyra commented on the Talk Show Host nomination afterward, saying:

> **The nomination was a surprise to me and I was thrilled! I know it's a cliché, but it really is gratifying to be recognized by my peers. I was on cloud nine for a week after I learned about the nomination. I always knew this is what I wanted to do, and the nomination is validation of that ambition. It's also flattering to be in the company of such talented nominees. I'm really ecstatic about it.**

The Ellen DeGeneres Show beat out Tyra's show in most of the categories, but just being nominated was a major achievement for a new show. *The Tyra Banks Show* did win two Daytime Emmy Awards, for Outstanding Achievement in Hairstyling and Outstanding Achievement in Makeup.

A WORLDWIDE BRAND

Tyra was extremely busy with her two television shows. She was making more than 170 episodes of her talk show per year and

Tyra Banks shares a laugh with *American Idol's* host, Ryan Seacrest, who is making a guest appearance on *The Tyra Banks Show.* Tyra's show draws a huge audience. Among women ages 18 to 34, around 2.2 million watch each week. The popular talk show has delivered the highest daytime ratings in years for stations in New York, Los Angeles, and Boston.

producing 13 new weekly episodes of *America's Next Top Model* every six months.

In addition, *America's Next Top Model* was airing in more than 100 countries. The U.S. version of the show was catching on in other countries as well. Tyra and producer Ken Mok worked with Viacom International to create *Top Model* spin-offs that were tailored to work with various countries and cultures. Some of the international versions of the show include *Slovakia's Next Top Supermodel, Italia's Next Top Model*, and *Afghanistan's Next Top Model*.

When *America's Next Top Model* debuted in September 2006 on The CW, it was the highest-rated series on the network and the

CROSS-CURRENTS

For information on how the Top Model winners have gone on to successful modeling careers, read "Where Are They Now?" Go to page 54. ▶▶

number-one show in average viewers. More than 5 million people watched each week during the 2006–2007 season, making it one of the longest running and most successful reality shows on TV.

⇒ SO WHAT! ⇐

In early 2007, something happened that would change Tyra's life and the course of her talk show. Someone snapped a photo of her in a bathing suit and sold it to the tabloids. These newspapers ran the unflattering photo accompanied by nasty headlines like "America's Next Top Waddle" and "Thigh-Ra Banks."

An episode from *The Tyra Banks Show* being filmed in Times Square, New York City. The show's style has been described as haphazard at times. There are no rehearsals for scenes taped in the studio, mistakes are acknowledged, and scenes are often improvised. By revealing her flaws, Tyra comes across to her audience as a real person, and not a supermodel celebrity.

Although Tyra was heavier than she had been at the peak of her modeling career, at five-feet, ten inches and 161 pounds she was far from fat. Her feelings were hurt by the negative publicity. She was also worried that the fuss over the photos would make other women feel bad about the way they looked or how much they weighed. Commenting on the issue later, Tyra said:

> **"I get so much mail from young girls who say, 'I look up to you, you're not as skinny as everyone else, I think you're beautiful.' So when they say that my body is 'ugly' and 'disgusting,' what does that make those girls feel like?"**

Deciding that she needed to fight back, Tyra tearfully and angrily addressed the issue on her talk show. She also organized a new campaign for the show in February called So What!

The So What! campaign was designed to inspire women to love themselves as they are. Most of the episodes that were part of the campaign focused on weight and body image. In one show, Tyra and her guests donned bathing suits and took turns announcing how much they weighed. In a post-show interview, Tyra explained why she launched the campaign:

> **"I was raised by women who don't believe that being super-skinny is the epitome of beauty. Being the best that you can be? That's beautiful, and I wanted to find a way to encourage every woman to love her body."**

≫ AWARD WINNER ≪

That same year, Tyra was honored with more than a half-dozen awards, including a Teen Choice Award for Favorite TV Personality. *People* magazine counted her as one of the 100 Most Beautiful People in the World and *Class-Elite Magazine* named her a Role Model for Models.

Tyra was also placed on *Time* magazine's list of the 100 Most Influential People in the World for the second year in a row. A few of the other people to make the list in 2007 included senator and presidential candidate Barack Obama, actor Leonardo DiCaprio,

Tyra's mentor Oprah Winfrey, and Pope Benedict XVI. In a short *Time* article, feminist author Naomi Wolf wrote:

> **Most of America sees Banks, 33, as a swimsuit model or a talk-show host. But very few see her as the latest in a line of African-American women entrepreneurs who have taken whatever it was they had to work with and turned it into an industry with aspirational overtones. We are lucky . . . that she believes what she is telling other girls and young women—that she is far, far more than just a body in a bathing suit.**

America's Next Top Model has stayed on the air longer than most reality shows. If viewer ratings are any indication, the show will be on for years to come. In 2008, The CW announced that the network would renew *America's Next Top Model* as long as it was successful.

In its third season, *The Tyra Banks Show* was renewed through 2009. The talk show is considered a powerhouse for The CW network.

⮞ CHANGING THE WORLD ⮜

One highlight of Tyra's career came at the end of 2007 and the beginning of 2008. It was the start of the presidential campaign season, and on her talk show she had an opportunity to interview many of the people who were running for president. Episodes showcased Democratic candidates John Edwards, Barack Obama, and Hillary Rodham Clinton and Republican candidate Mike Huckabee.

The interviews were a mix of serious questions and lighthearted fun. For example, Tyra asked Hillary Clinton about political scandals, then switched over to the topic of cellulite. When she interviewed Barack Obama, she grilled him about his political policies and then cheerfully invited herself over to the White House. She later told *Entertainment Weekly* about the challenge of doing a serious interview but still being true to her show:

> **It was a lot of pressure. It felt like people were going to be watching in a different way. It made me feel like I can't just look like a dumb model. But this is not CNN either, so I still have to be fun and quirky and cute and girly.**

BLACK ENTERPRISE

YOUR ULTIMATE GUIDE TO
FINANCIAL EMPOWERMENT

30 Great Franchises

SEPTEMBER 2006

Models Inc.
TYRA & IMAN
Fashion Icons
Succeeding As
Entrepreneurs

Top 50
Colleges
For African
Americans

B.E. Corporate
Executive
Of The Year
Aetna's
Ron Williams

The September 2006 cover of *Black Enterprise* magazine features supermodels Tyra and Iman—but its focus is on how both have become savvy businesswomen. In a story entitled "Models Inc.," Tyra receives praise for successfully hosting and producing two popular television programs, while Iman is noted for establishing a cosmetics empire that sells millions of dollars of products each year.

Tyra Banks is honored for her media work throughout her career by Black Entertainment Television (BET) at the BET Honors event held in Washington, D.C., on January 12, 2008. The following June she would take home another coveted award. That month *The Tyra Banks Show* won the Emmy in a new category, Outstanding Talk Show—Informative.

Although her interviews of the presidential candidates are among her proudest accomplishments to date, Tyra says that she still has a lot to do. The focus of her career has evolved from trying to get on the cover of a magazine to trying to change the world. In the third season of her talk show, Tyra committed herself to this new goal by developing episodes that were meant to inspire other people. She visited inner-city high schools, planted trees in New York, and continued to address issues central to women.

Tyra also changed the mission statement of her TZONE Foundation to help even more young women. Her number-one priority is empowering as many people as possible.

➤ WHAT THE FUTURE HOLDS ◀

Tyra has been working in the entertainment industry for more than 20 years. She has become one of the most accomplished and influential people on television, and she shows no signs of slowing down anytime soon.

Tyra recently signed a long-term production deal with Warner Bros. Television to develop projects under the banner of "Tyra Banks Presents." She has several movies and TV shows in the works. Tyra is also developing straight-to-DVD movies based on the bestselling Clique series of books. Some of the other projects she has mentioned pursuing include Broadway shows, an amusement park, another fashion-related reality show, and various online enterprises. Tyra has explained that her underlying concept for all of these projects is to be fun while also helping young women feel more confident and able to take control over their lives:

> **"It's the attainable fantasy. Girl empowerment—but not preachy. I like it to be surrounded by a little bit of candy so you don't know that you're getting a message."**

Whatever Tyra Banks decides to do in the future, she will almost certainly continue to inspire people around the world.

America's Next Top Model Goes International

Created and coproduced by Tyra Banks, the Australian version of America's Next Top Model *has also been broadcast in the United States by the VH1 network. The panel of judges from an early season of* Australia's Next Top Model *are, from left to right, former managing magazine editor Marguerite Kramer, stylist Ken Thompson, model/presenter Erika Heynatz, and fashion designer Alex Perry.*

America's Next Top Model has become an international phenomenon, and versions of Tyra's show air in more than 30 different countries. Some of these countries include:

Afghanistan—*Afghanistan's Next Top Model*
Aruba—*Aruba Model Search*
Australia—*Australia's Next Top Model*
Belgium—*Top Model Belgium*
Brazil—*Brazil's Next Top Model*
Canada—*Canada's Next Top Model*
Caribbean—*Caribbean's Next Top Model*
Central America—*Super Model Centroamerica*
China—*China's Next Top Model*
Croatia—*Hrvatski Top Model*
Denmark—*Denmark's Next Top Model*
Finland—*Searching for Finland's Top Model*
France—*France's Next Top Model*
Germany—*Germany's Next Top Model*
Ghana—*Top Model Ghana*
Honduras—*Amiga Top Model*

Hungary—*Hungary's Next Top Model*
Israel—*The Models*
Italy—*Italia's Next Top Model*
The Netherlands—*Holland's Next Top Model*
Nigeria—*Nigeria's Next Top Model*
Norway—*Norway's Next Top Model*
Philippines—*Philippines' Next Top Model*
Russia—*Russia's Next Top Model*
Scandinavia—*Scandinavia's Next Top Model*
Slovakia—*Slovakia's Next Top Supermodel*
Spain—*Supermodelo*
Sweden—*Sweden's Next Top Supermodel*
Switzerland—*Switzerland's Next Supermodel*
Taiwan—*Taiwan Supermodel No. 1*
Thailand—*Thailand's Next Top Model*
United Kingdom—*Britain's Next Top Model*

(Go back to page 7.) ◀◀

Filming in New York City

New York City is often called the "Talk Show Capital of the World" because so many talk shows are filmed there. Besides *The Tyra Banks Show*, other major talk shows that are filmed in New York include:

- *Good Morning America*
- *Late Night with Conan O'Brien*
- *Live with Regis and Kelly*
- *Rachael Ray*
- *The Colbert Report*

- *The Daily Show*
- *The Early Show*
- *The Late Show with David Letterman*
- *The Today Show*
- *The View*
- *Total Request Live (TRL)*

But New York is not just home to talk shows. Many other kinds of television programs are filmed in studios or on location in the city. Some past and present shows include:

- *30 Rock*
- *All My Children*
- *Another World*
- *As the World Turns*
- *Car 54, Where Are You?*
- *Guiding Light*
- *Hope and Faith*
- *Kate and Allie*
- *Law & Order*
- *Law & Order: Criminal Intent*
- *Law & Order: Special Victims Unit*
- *Law & Order: Trial by Jury*
- *New York Undercover*
- *One Life to Live*
- *Rescue Me*
- *Saturday Night Live*
- *Sesame Street*
- *Sex and the City*
- *Spin City*
- *The Black Donnellys*
- *The Cosby Show*
- *The Equalizer*
- *The Tonight Show*
- *Third Watch*
- *Who Wants to Be a Millionaire?*

An episode from the weekday news show Good Morning America *is taped on the streets of New York City. The television program, produced live from Times Square Studios, features news, talk, weather, and special interest stories. Hosts for the program, which launched in 1975, have included David Hartman, Joan Lunden, Charlie Gibson, Diane Sawyer, and Robin Roberts.*

(Go back to page 9.)

Other African-American Supermodels: Past and Present

Tyra is not the only successful African-American supermodel. There have been several other black models who have enjoyed success on the runway and in magazines or advertising campaigns. Some of the most notable African-American supermodels include:

Born in May 1970, British supermodel Naomi Campbell is of African, Jamaican, and Chinese descent. In addition to being a model, Campbell has appeared in television, music videos, and film. Her company, the Design House of Naomi Campbell, which she founded in 1999, sells cosmetics, shower gels, and perfume fragrances.

Donyale Luna

Born Peggy Anne Freeman, Donyale Luna modeled during the 1960s and 1970s. She was the first African-American model to appear on the cover of British *Vogue* (in 1966) and is often referred to as the first African-American cover girl. Donyale also acted in a number of films, including several by artist Andy Warhol.

Naomi Campbell

Naomi Campbell is a British supermodel who began modeling in 1986 and still models today. She was the first African-American model to appear on the cover of the fashion magazine *Vogue* Paris and the weekly newsmagazine *Time*.

Liya Kebede

Liya Kebede, an Ethiopian-born model, is one of the highest-paid models in the industry today. In addition to modeling for runway shows and magazines, she has been the face for several ad campaigns. Liya recently signed a groundbreaking contract with Estée Lauder, becoming the first black model in the company's history.

(Go back to page 12.)

Crossing Over into Acting

Tyra was lucky and talented enough to cross over from modeling into acting. Some others who have had similar success making the move from fashion modeling to other areas of the entertainment industry include:

Cameron Diaz

After working as a fashion model for five years, Cameron Diaz auditioned for and obtained her first major movie role. She went on to star in more than 30 movies and has become one of the highest-paid actresses in Hollywood.

Katie Price

Katie Price, also known as Jordan, is a former glamour model who has managed to make a small fortune in a variety of different industries. She is an accomplished author, designer, singer, and most recently, a reality television star.

Kimora Lee Simmons

Kimora Lee Simmons went from model to mogul. She launched a fashion line in 1999, wrote a best-selling book in 2006, and had a Barbie doll made in her likeness in 2007. Kimora has also worked as an actress and a TV show host.

Milla Jovovich

Milla Jovovich began modeling at the age of 11. Since then, she has appeared in

A year older than Tyra, born August 30, 1972, Cameron Diaz began her career at age 16 as a fashion model. Like Tyra, she signed with Elite Model Management and modeled for several years. In 1994, she auditioned for and won the lead female role in the comedy film The Mask. *Since then, the award-winning actress has appeared in numerous movies.*

hundreds of magazines and ad campaigns. Her modeling eventually led to major movie roles and several award nominations. Milla has also enjoyed success as a folk singer and fashion designer.

(Go back to page 15.)

Tyra's TZONE

Tyra created the TZONE Foundation in 1999 to provide summer camps for girls in southern California. The foundation changed its focus in 2006 from offering camps to making grants to empower women. Today, TZONE awards grants to nonprofit organizations that serve women and girls between the ages of 13 and 35.

Some of the organizations the foundation has helped fund include Young Chicago Authors, the Ifetayo Cultural Arts Facility, the Lower Eastside Girls Club, the Downtown Women's Center (DWC) of Los Angeles, Girls in the Game, and the Sadie Nash Leadership Project.

The TZONE Foundation's Web site says that its primary mission is to build a sisterhood movement among women and girls. By making grants available to community-based non-profits, Tyra and the rest of the foundation staff hope to encourage philanthropy and raise awareness for women's issues.

To explain why she started TZONE, Tyra published this message on the TZONE Web site:

"I started TZONE with my own money because I feel I have a responsibility to raise the awareness of the needs, ambitions and accomplishments of women and girls and to encourage others to join me in funding outstanding community-based organizations that help women live into their full potential."

(Go back to page 20.)

Getting to Know Oprah

Oprah Winfrey is a **philanthropist**, book critic, producer, publisher, actress, and talk show host. She is the first African-American woman to become a billionaire. Because of her enormous media empire, some people consider her the most influential woman in the world.

Oprah has overcome great hardships, including extreme poverty and racial discrimination, to get where she is today. After graduating from high school, Oprah won the Miss Black Tennessee beauty pageant. She later graduated from Tennessee State University and began a career as a television news anchor.

In 1983 Oprah moved to Chicago to take over a talk show that was struggling in the ratings. Within a few months it was the most popular talk show in Chicago, and by 1986 the program was broadcast nationally. Since then, *The Oprah Winfrey Show* has become the highest-rated talk show in history. Nearly 50 million American viewers watch the show each week, and it is broadcast in more than 134 countries.

Oprah has always been one of Tyra's role models. In a recent interview, Tyra acknowledged the influence Oprah has had on her life:

"Oprah is definitely a mentor, because she is the best at what she does and she has such an amazing heart and spirit. She's a constant source of inspiration for me."

(Go back to page 22.)

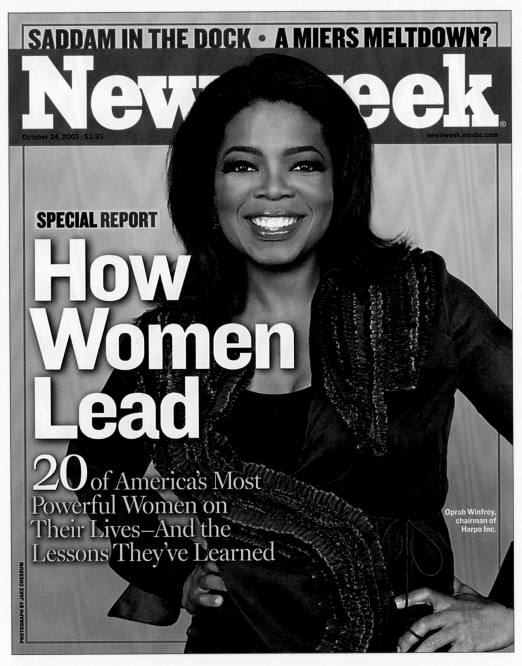

The October 24, 2005, issue of Newsweek features Oprah Winfrey on its cover. Tyra, who apprenticed on Winfrey's show for two seasons, considers Oprah her mentor. On June 20, 2008, when Tyra received her first Emmy—for Outstanding Talk Show in the Informative category, she said, "I want to thank Oprah Winfrey for her inspiration. She is the queen. She will always be the queen."

Tyra's Work Behind the Camera

As a model, actress, and TV show host, Tyra is frequently in the spotlight. But she also does a lot of work behind the camera. Tyra is the executive producer of both *America's Next Top Model* and *The Tyra Banks Show*. She has also coproduced several episodes of the spinoff *Australia's Next Top Model*.

For every hour Tyra spends oncamera, she spends an average of three hours behind the scenes doing research, writing, editing, and making decisions on everything from graphics to camera shots. Some of her other duties as a producer include monitoring budgets and choosing who will be involved with her on different projects.

On several occasions, Tyra has said that at first people underestimated her abilities as a producer. However, her hands-on style and knack for making good choices have earned her the respect of many industry veterans.

In addition, Tyra is constantly working to develop new television shows and movies through her company, Bankable Productions. She has made it her mission to create concepts that promote the idea of self-empowerment as well as feature female characters who are good role models.

(Go back to page 30.)

Bankable Productions' head and America's Next Top Model *executive producer Tyra Banks works behind the camera during the shooting of an episode for her model search show. Since founding her own production company in 2003 (which she originally named Ty Ty Baby after her childhood nickname), Tyra has successfully created a media empire.*

Other Women's Talk Shows

A scene from the September 8, 2003, premiere episode of The Ellen DeGeneres Show, *which featured actress Jennifer Aniston (left). The daytime talk show has continued to increase in popularity and as of 2008 has earned its host recognition with 10 Emmy Awards, including Outstanding Talk Show and Outstanding Talk Show Host.*

Tyra Banks is one of several women who have hosted very successful talk shows. Some other notable talk show hosts include Barbara Walters, Ellen DeGeneres, Oprah Winfrey, and Rachael Ray.

Barbara Walters is the co-creator and co-host of *The View*, a popular daytime talk show. *The View* features a panel of female hosts from different generations and different backgrounds who interview celebrities and discuss "hot topics" in a roundtable-style forum.

Considered by many to be one of the funniest women alive, Ellen DeGeneres has been the host of *The Ellen DeGeneres Show* since 2003. This daytime talk show, which is a blend of comedy, celebrity interviews, and human-interest stories, has been nominated for dozens of awards and averages 3 million viewers per episode.

Oprah Winfrey started out as a news anchor and ended up a talk show host. Her program, *The Oprah Winfrey Show*, is the highest-rated talk show in television history. Oprah's guests typically include celebrities and individuals who have been involved in extraordinary situations.

After hosting a number of well-received shows on the Food Network, Rachael Ray inked a deal with Oprah Winfrey and King World Productions to host her own daytime talk show. *Rachael Ray* has since become one of the top-ranked daytime programs on television.

(Go back to page 34.)

Where Are They Now?

Following are the names of the models who have won the title of America's Next Top Model, and a little about their careers after the show:

Season One—Adrianne Curry

Adrianne is arguably one of the most successful winners of *America's Next Top Model*. She has scored numerous modeling gigs and has even starred in several of her own reality shows since winning the season-one title.

Season Two—Yoanna House

After beating out the other contestants in season two, Yoanna worked as a runway model for Custo Barcelona, Sue Wong, and other designers. She has also hosted a few TV shows, including *The Look for Less* and *Queen Bees*.

Season Three—Eva Pigford

Eva Pigford, who now goes by the name of Eva Marcille, graced the covers of a half-dozen magazines after winning the title. She has also guest starred on several television series and recently hosted a couple of reality shows.

Season Four—Naima Mora

Naima has modeled for dozens of magazines and runway shows since winning season four. She also appeared in commercials and music videos. Most recently, she released an album with her band, Chewing Pics.

Season Five—Nicole Linkletter

After winning season five, Nicole modeled for magazines like *Elle*, *Lemonade Magazine*, and *Celebrity Living*. She also appeared in advertisements for CoverGirl Cosmetics, PlayStation Portable, and Vigoss.

Season Six—Danielle Evans

Danielle has modeled steadily in magazines and runway shows since winning the title. Most recently, she was named the spokesperson for the Akademics clothing line.

Season Seven—CariDee English

CariDee has been an in-demand model since beating out the other contestants in season seven. She has modeled for CoverGirl Cosmetics and several high-profile magazines. CariDee was also signed as the spokesperson for the National Psoriasis Foundation.

Season Eight—Jaslene Gonzalez

Since winning the title in season eight, Jaslene has embarked on a successful modeling career, appearing in a number of magazines and ad campaigns. She also had a small role in the movie *Humboldt Park*.

Season Nine—Saleisha Stowers

After winning season nine, Saleisha appeared on the cover of several major magazines, including *Seventeen* and *Paper Doll Magazine*. She has also participated on the runway in numerous fashion shows.

Season Ten—Whitney Thompson

The popular Whitney became a finalist for a Teen Choice Award, under Female Reality/Variety star. When Whitney was selected, it was the first time a top model had ever been nominated.

(Go back to page 40.)

★ America's Next Top Model WINNER! ★
that's Her! ↘

seventeen

250+ fun things to do!
- 5-Minute Makeovers
- Spring-Break Discounts
- Date Ideas He'll Love

February 2007

INTRODUCING...
America's Next Top Model
cariDee
"This Is What I'm Meant To Do—It's A Great Feeling"

HOT HAIRCUTS
The Best Cheap & Chic Salons Near You

Love
Make Your Ex Want You Back!

FREE T-SHIRT
Exclusively From Aéropostale!

17 REAL LIFE
"I Lied Online To Get Attention"

The seventh season winner of American's Next Top Model, CariDee English appears on the February 2007 cover of Seventeen magazine. Being featured in the magazine was part of the prize for winning ANTM in December 2006. She also received a $100,000 contract with CoverGirl Cosmetics and a contract with Elite Model Management.

Selected Highlights

1973 Tyra Lynne Banks is born on December 4 in Inglewood, California.

1990 At the age of 17, Tyra signs a modeling contract with Elite Modeling Management.

1991 During her first two weeks as a model, Tyra receives a record 25 runway bookings.

1992 Tyra establishes the Tyra Banks Scholarship, which gives African-American girls the opportunity to attend Tyra's former school, Immaculate Heart High School, in Los Angeles.

1995 Tyra signs a lucrative spokesperson contract with the cosmetics company CoverGirl.

1996 Tyra becomes the first African-American model to appear on the cover of *Victoria's Secret* catalog, *GQ*, and *Sports Illustrated's* swimsuit issue.

1998 *Tyra's Beauty Inside and Out* is published by Harper Perennial.

1999 Tyra creates the TZONE Foundation and begins working as a youth correspondent for the *Oprah Winfrey Show*.

2003 Tyra establishes her own company, Bankable Productions.

America's Next Top Model premiers on the UPN network and becomes a hit.

2005 Tyra launches a daytime talk show in September.

In December, after participating in a final fashion show for Victoria's Secret, Tyra retires from modeling.

2007 *The Tyra Banks Show* moves to New York City.

2008 In January, Black Entertainment Television honors Tyra for her lifetime of accomplishments in the media.

In June, Tyra receives her first Emmy, from the Academy of Television Arts and Sciences.

Television Credits

1992 *Inferno*
1993 *Fresh Prince of Bel-Air*
1997 *New York Undercover*
1999 *Felicity*
The Hughleys
Just Shoot Me
2000 *Mad TV*
2001 *Soul Food*
2003 *America's Next Top Model*
2004 *All of Us*
American Dreams
America's Next Top Model
2005 *The Tyra Banks Show*
America's Next Top Model
2006 *America's Next Top Model*
The Tyra Banks Show
2007 *America's Next Top Model*
The Tyra Banks Show
2008 *America's Next Top Model*
The Tyra Banks Show

Music Video Credits

1991 Michael Jackson's *Black or White*
Tina Turner's *Love Thing*
1992 George Michael's *Too Funky*
1995 Mobb Deep's *Trife Life*
2004 Tyra Banks's *Shake Ya Body*

Movie Credits

1994 *Extra Terrorestrial Alien Encounter*
Supermodels in the Rainforest
1995 *Higher Learning*
1997 *A Woman Like That*
1999 *The Apartment Complex*
Love Stinks
2000 *Coyote Ugly*
Life-Size
Love & Basketball

2001 *Larceny*
2002 *Eight Crazy Nights*
         Halloween: Resurrection
2007 *Mr. Woodcock*

Producing Credits
2003 *America's Next Top Model*
2004 *America's Next Top Model*
         Australia's Next Top Model
2005 *America's Next Top Model*
2006 *America's Next Top Model*
2007 *America's Next Top Model*
2008 *The Tyra Banks Show*

Selected Awards
1994 *People Magazine*'s 50 Most Beautiful People
1996 *People Magazine*'s 50 Most Beautiful People
1997 Michael Award for Supermodel of the Year
         VH1 Supermodel of the Year
2000 *Sports Illustrated* Woman of the Year
2006 *Time Magazine*'s 100 Most Influential People
         Time Magazine's 100 People Who Shape Our World
2007 *Class-Elite Magazine's* Role Model for Models
         People Magazine's 100 Most Beautiful People in the World
         Teen Choice Award
         Time Magazine's 100 Most Influential People
2008 BET Media Award
         Emmy Award, Outstanding Talk Show/Informative

Books

Banks, Tyra, and Vanessa Thomas Bush. *Tyra's Beauty Inside and Out*. New York: Harper Perennial, 1998.

Chase, Lila. *Totally Tyra: An Unauthorized Biography*. New York: Price Stern Sloan, 2006.

Hill, Anne E. *Tyra Banks: From Supermodel to Role Model*. Minneapolis: Lerner, 2009.

Iman with Tina Williams. *The Beauty of Color*. New York: Penguin Group, 2006.

Mitchell, Susan K. *Tyra Banks*. Strongsville, Ohio: Gareth Stevens, 2007.

Summers, Barbara. *Black and Beautiful: How Women of Color Changed the Fashion Industry*. Darby: Diane Publishing, 2003

Web Sites

http://tyrabanks.com

Tyra Banks's official Web site includes photo galleries, videos, free downloads, and information about Tyra's television shows and other projects.

http://tzonefoundation.org

The official Web site of Tyra's TZONE foundation features information about the foundation's mission, projects, and grants.

http://tyrashow.warnerbros.com/

The official Web site of *The Tyra Banks Show* features show recaps, galleries, and details about Tyra's world.

http://www.cwtv.com/shows/americas-next-top-model

The official Web site for *America's Next Top Model* includes photos, interviews, full episodes, a fan lounge, and much more.

http://www.people.com/people/tyra_banks

People Magazine's official Web site features Tyra photos and a bio, as well as regular news updates.

Publisher's note:
The Web sites mentioned in this book were active at the time of publication. The publisher is not responsible for Web sites that have changed their addresses or discontinued operation since the date of publication. The publisher will review and update the Web site addresses each time the book is reprinted.

catwalk—a long, narrow raised platform or walkway used by models in fashion shows.

contract—a formal legal document that sets out the terms of an agreement between two or more people.

controversial—causing a strong reaction, disagreement, or debate.

correspondent—a news reporter or commentator.

executive producer—an individual who supervises the production, distribution, and promotion of an entertainment project.

lingerie—fashionable women's undergarments.

lucrative—profitable.

mogul—a powerful or influential businessperson.

nomination—the act of naming someone as a finalist for an award.

philanthropist—an individual who does good deeds and charitable work.

pitch—to try to sell or promote something, such as a business venture.

portfolio—a collection of pictures that show off a model's work.

runway—a platform or walkway used by models in fashion shows.

scholarship—a monetary award given to students to finance education costs.

spokesperson—a company representative.

supermodel—term for a model who has become internationally successful and is in high demand by fashion designers and photographers.

unprecedented—having never happened before.

page 6 "Even as a model . . . " Tim Stack, "America's Next Top Mogul," *Entertainment Weekly* (February 22, 2008), p. 28.

page 6 "I understood that people . . . " Ray Richmond, "Tyra Banks Is Proud of Her Success and Looking for More," *The Hollywood Reporter* (March 4, 2008). http://www.venturacountystar.com/news/2008/mar/04/model-to-mogul.

page 9 Moving the talk show . . . " Natalie Finn, "Tyra Takes New York," E! Online (2008). http://www.eonline.com/news/article/index.jsp?uuid=359e5f28-1c28-43f6-828e-c2d32acdb0d4.

page 11 "I admit I did fantasize . . . " Tyra Banks, with Vanessa Thomas Bush, *Tyra's Beauty Inside and Out* (New York: Harper Perennial, 1998), p. 168.

page 12 "The market for black . . . " Tom Gliatto and Bryan Alexander, "Tyrasaurus! Tyra Banks, a Top Model, Is Raring to Reign as an Actress," *People* 41, no. 13 (April 11, 1994), p. 57.

page 18 "I truly get so . . . " Banks and Bush, *Tyra's Beauty Inside and Out*, p. 184.

page 20 "I tell the girls . . . " Judy Dutton and Jeannie Kim, "Mothers & Shakers 2002!" *Redbook* 199, no. 4 (October 2002), p. 118.

page 21 "There are a million . . . " Banks and Bush, *Tyra's Beauty Inside and Out*, p. 13.

page 28 "It was kind of . . . " "'Model' Making," *Entertainment Weekly* 979 (February 22, 2008), p. 34.

page 31 "I've been singing for . . . " Joyce Wadler et al., "Boldface Names," New York Times (February 18, 2004), p. C1.

page 33 "She's really emerged as . . . " "Tyra Banks Tilts Toward Talk Show," Knight Ridder/Tribune News Service (October 1, 2004). http://www.accessmylibrary.com/coms2/summary_0286-6252093_ITM.

page 33 "I thought I was . . . " Juan Morales, "Tyra Banks: The Supermodel-Turned-TV Host Tells It Like She Sees It—And She Doesn't Miss Much," *Redbook* 206, no. 4 (April 2006), p. 136.

page 34 "I'm not just retiring . . . " Samantha Critchell, "A Model No More: Tyra Banks Retires," Associated Press (December 7, 2005). http://seattletimes.nwsource.com/html/living/2002668284_tyra07.html.

page 38 "For the first season . . . " Aldore D. Collier, "Tyra Banks: Success as Fashion Model and Businesswoman Makes Her a Role Model as Well," *Jet* 110, no. 17 (October 30, 2006), p. 60.

page 38 "The nomination was a . . . " Waldman, "Personal Touch Makes Tyra Unique," p. 24.

page 41 "I get so much . . . " Allison Adato, "Tyra Talks," *People* 67, no. 5 (February 5, 2007), p. 82.

page 41 "I was raised by . . . " Claire Connors, "'Why I Love My Body ... Just the Way It Is': Tyra Banks Is Here to Prove You're as Beautiful as You Feel, No Matter What You Weigh," *Shape* 26, no. 10 (June 2007), p. 63.

page 42 "Most of America . . ." Naomi Wolf, "Tyra Banks," *Time* 169, no. 20 (May 14, 2007), p. 80.

page 42 "It was a lot of pressure . . ." Stack, "America's Next Top Mogul," p. 28.

page 45 "It's the attainable fantasy . . ." Stack, "America's Next Top Mogul," p. 28.

page 50 "I started TZONE with . . . " Tyra Banks, "Message From Tyra," TZONE Foundation Web Site. http://tzonefoundation.org/message.html.

page 50 "Oprah is definitely a . . . " Allison J. Waldman, "Personal Touch Makes Tyra Unique: As She Grows in Host Role, Banks Is Learning from Her Audience How to Serve Them," *Television Week* 26, no. 17 (April 23, 2007), p. 24.

America's Next Top Model, 4, 6–8, 26–30, *31*, 34, 36–37, 39–40, 42, 52, 54–55
  international spin-offs, 39, 46
The Apartment Complex (movie), 22

Bankable Enterprises, 5
Bankable Productions, 5, 30, 34, 52
Banks, Devin (brother), 11–12
Banks, Donald (father), 11–12
Banks, Tyra
  and acting, 15, 17, 22–23, *24*, 25, 49
  and *America's Next Top Model, 4*, 6–8, 26–30, *31*, 34, 36–37, 39–40, 42, 46, 52, 54–55
  awards won by, 18, 38, 41–42, *44*
  birth and childhood, 10–12
  and body image, *10*, 12, 40–41, 42
  and books, 20–22
  and business ventures, 5–6, 30, 34–35, 38–39, *43*, 45, 52
  and charity work, 18–20, 45, 50
  and dating, 9, 15, 25, 33
  and modeling, 5, 6, 12–18, 23–25, 34–35
  and music career, 30–31, 33
  and race, 12, *14*, 15
  and *The Tyra Banks Show,* 8–9, *32*, 33–34, 37–39, *40*, 42, *44*, 45, 47, 53
  and Victoria's Secret, 15, 23–25, 34–35
Barker, Nigel, 30
Bush, Vanessa Thomas, 20

Campbell, Naomi, 48
charity work, 18–20, 45, 50

CoverGirl, *14*, 15, 22
Coyote Ugly (movie), 23
Curry, Adrianne, 30, 54

Daytime Emmy Awards, 9, 38
DeGeneres, Ellen, 38, 53
Diaz, Cameron, 49
Dickinson, Janice, 28, 30

Eight Crazy Nights (movie), 25
Elite Model Management, 13, 15

The Fresh Prince of Bel-Air (TV show), 15

Halloween: Resurrection (movie), *24*, 25
Higher Learning (movie), 15
House, Yoanna, 30, 54

Immaculate Heart Middle and High School, 12, 19–20

Jenkins, Alexander ("J. Alexander"), *31*
Jovovich, Milla, 49

Kebede, Liya, 48

Life-Size (movie), 22–23
London-Johnson, Carolyn (mother), 5, 6, 11–12, *13*, 15
Love & Basketball (movie), 22
Love Stinks (movie), 22
Luna, Donyale, 48

Manuel, Jay, *29*
Michael Award for Supermodel of the Year, 18
Mok, Ken, 27, 28, 39

New York City, N.Y., 9, 47
New York Undercover (TV show), 17

Nicholson, Eric, 30

Obama, Barack, 42
The Oprah Winfrey Show (TV show), 22, *32*, 33, 50–51
Ostroff, Dawn, 28

Paratore, Jim, 33
Price, Katie, 49

Quillian, Beau, 28, 30

Ray, Rachael, 53

Seal, 25
"Shake Ya Body" (song), 30–31, 33
Simmons, Kimora Lee, 28, 30, 49
Singleton, John, 15, 25
So What! campaign, 41
Sports Illustrated, 14, 15
Supermodel. See America's Next Top Model

The Tyra Banks Show (TV show), 8–9, *32*, 33–34, 37–39, *40*, 42, *44*, 45, 47, 53
Tyra's Beauty Inside and Out (book), 20–22
TZONE Foundation, 20, 45, 50

Utendahl, John, 9

Victoria's Secret, 15, 23–25, 34–35

Walters, Barbara, 53
Webber, Chris, 25, 33
Winfrey, Oprah, 22, *32*, 33, 42, 50–51, 53
Wolf, Naomi, 42
A Woman Like That (movie), 17

Karen Schweitzer has written numerous articles for magazines, newspapers, and Web sites like About.com. She has also authored several books for young adults, including biographies of Shaun White, Sheryl Swoopes, and Soulja Boy Tell 'Em for the MODERN ROLE MODELS series. Karen lives in Michigan with her husband. You can learn more about her at www.karenschweitzer.com.

PICTURE CREDITS

page

1: Starstock/PRMS

4: Lester Cohen Archive/WireImage

7: The CW Network/NMI

8: thepopculturejunkie/CIC Photos

10: London Features Int'l-UMA

13: London Features Int'l

14: P.O.V./NMI

16: Vision in BLACK/NMI

19: London Features Int'l

21: HarperPerennial/NMI

23: Marion Curtis/StartraksPhoto

24: Dimension Films/FilmMagic

26: Ace Pictures

29: The CW Network/PRMS

31: CBS/KRT

32: In New York/NMI

35: Victoria's Secret/NMI

36: The CW Network/PRMS

39: Warner Bros/PRMS

40: cracked22/CIC Photos

43: Black Enterprise/NMI

44: Scott Gries/Getty Images

46: VH1/FOX8/PRMS

47: shutterberry/T&T/IOA Photos

48: Fashion Wire Daily

49: AdMedia/Sipa Press

51: Newsweek/NMI

52: The CW Network/PRMS

53: NBC/NMI

55: Seventeen/NMI

Front cover: CBS/PRMS